Senses

Touching and Feeling

Author's Note

I have worked alongside young children for more than forty years.
Over this period I have learned never to be surprised at their perceptive
comments about the physical world in which they live. Many of their
observations ("Have you seen the crinkles in the elephant's trunk?"
"How do seeds know which is their top and which is their bottom?")
indicate keen observation and an intuitive use of the senses of taste,
touch, sight, smell, and hearing.

The sense-dependent nature of the young child should come as no
surprise to parents and teachers. In the early years of life images
provided by the senses shape our interpretation of our surroundings
and lay the foundations upon which subsequent learning is built.
The ideas of hot and cold, far and near, quiet and loud, sweet and sour,
soft and hard are developed through the interaction of the child with his
or her immediate environment. This interaction encourages observation
and questioning which in turn leads to talk and the extension and
deepening of language.

This book (like its companions in the series) is a picture book which seeks
to encourage both looking and talking. The text may be read by child or
adult. Alternatively it may be ignored, the pictures alone being used to
trigger an exploration of the child's own insights.

Published by Raintree Steck-Vaughn Publishers, an
imprint of Steck-Vaughn Company, a subsidiary of
Harcourt Brace & Company

Editors: Helen Lanz, Shirley Shalit
Art Director: Robert Walster
Project Manager: Gino Coverty
Designer: Kirstie Billingham
Photo Researcher: Sarah Snashall

Library of Congress Cataloging-in-Publication Data
Pluckrose, Henry Arthur.
Touching and feeling / by Henry Pluckrose.
   p. cm. -- (Senses)
Summary: Introduces the basic concept of touch and
how it affects our lives.
ISBN: 0-8172-5227-4
1. Touch--Juvenile liturature. [1. Touch. 2. Senses and
sensation.] I. Title. II. Series: Pluckrose, Henry Arthur.
Senses.
QP451.P584 1998
612.8'8--dc21
                                        97-30961
                                            CIP
                                            AC
Printed in Malaysia and bound in the United States
1 2 3 4 5 6 7 8 9 0 LB 01 00 99 98 97

Picture credits
Commissioned photography by Steve Shott: cover, 4, 5. Researched photography: Bruce Coleman Ltd 14
(P. Clement), 22 & 29 (J. Burton); Hutchinson Library 17 (L. Taylor); The Image Bank 7 (H. de Lespinasse), 8
(G. Obremski), 9 (R. M. Horowitz), 26-27 (I. Royd), 31 (D. W. Hamilton); James Davis Photography 12-13; Robert
Harding Picture Library 18 (G. Hellier), 20; Franklin Watts title page; Zefa 10, 11, 15, 19, 23, 25 (K&H Benser).

Senses

Touching and Feeling

by Henry Pluckrose

RSVP

RAINTREE
STECK-VAUGHN
P U B L I S H E R S

The Steck-Vaughn Company

Austin, Texas

We touch things with
our hands and our bodies.
The sense of touch
helps us to understand
the world in which we live.

Some things feel dry
and rough to touch,
like a crumbling old wall,
or sand dried by the sun.

Some things feel smooth,
like polished wood,
stones and pebbles
rounded by the sea,
the speckled shell
of a hen's egg.

Some things are soft
to the touch, like
cats' fur, cotton puffs,
a cuddly toy.

Some things are hard
to the touch.
Why do we use
hard materials to
build our houses, schools,
factories, and shops?

Some things are painful
to touch—
the prickles of a holly bush,
thorns on rose stems,
the needle-sharp spines
of a cactus.

People who are blind
are taught to read
through their sense of touch.
They feel the raised dots
on the paper with
the tips of their fingers.
Blind people learn that
each group of dots stands
for a certain letter of the alphabet.
Some groups even stand
for whole words.

We all use our fingers to learn.
Our sense of touch
tells us if something is hot
or cold, rough or smooth,
soft or hard.

Imagine. If you touched these things,
what would your hands
tell you?

What things do you most enjoy touching? Is it the soft, squashy feel of modeling clay? Is it the wet, slippery feel of finger paints?

Perhaps you like the feel
of things that move.
They touch you
when you touch them.
Things like running water,
a friendly animal,
or a big, bouncing ball.

We use our sense of touch
to give messages. A mother
cuddles her baby and
each feels a message of love.
When we shake hands to greet
a visitor, we send a friendly
message. We kiss to say hello
or goodbye. We touch to
give comfort.

This girl can feel the water and sand all over her body.
It feels good.
Sometimes people get hurt.
They may feel pain.
That is not a good feeling.

Nearly all animals
have the sense of touch.
These puppies' eyes have
not yet opened.
They cannot see their mother,
but they feel the warmth
and comfort of her body.

Often our senses
work together.
We feel the wet
sea breeze in our face.
We may hear, taste,
see, and smell it, too!

Investigations

This book has been prepared to encourage the young user to think about the sense of touch. Each picture spread creates an opportunity for talk. Sharing talk with a sympathetic adult plays an important part in the development of a child's understanding of the world. Through the subtlety of language, ideas are formed, questioned, and developed.

The photographs and supporting text concentrate on experiences common to most children—the softness of cats' fur, the cold, slimy feel of hand paints, the smoothness of glass or pebbles, the roughness of a tree's bark.

The theme of touch might be explored through questions and activities like these:

✦ Encouraging a child to explain how things "feel" in words makes a significant contribution to his/her language development. A simple way of uniting touch and language is through a "feeling bag"— a cloth with a pull-string opening. Into the bag (and unseen by the child) put a variety of small objects, e.g., a metal key, a coin, a swatch of fabric, a wrapped candy, a plastic comb. Invite the child to put his/her hands into the bag and to describe each object in turn. What are they made of? What are they used for? What gave you the clue to their use? How many things can you say about the objects just by touching them? What things can't you tell about them? This game can be played many times— though its long-term success depends on finding objects that intrigue.

✦ Discussion could include the concept that the sense of "feeling" also involves things that the child cannot see or touch directly—like warmth from sunlight.

✦ Another important aspect of the sense of touch is that it does not only relate to hands—the whole of the body is touch-sensitive.

✦ The way our senses work together can also be explored. What do we see that tells us that the frozen peas will feel cold to touch or that the water running into the bath is hot? If we can see heat and cold, can we also "smell" heat, "taste" cold—or hear them?